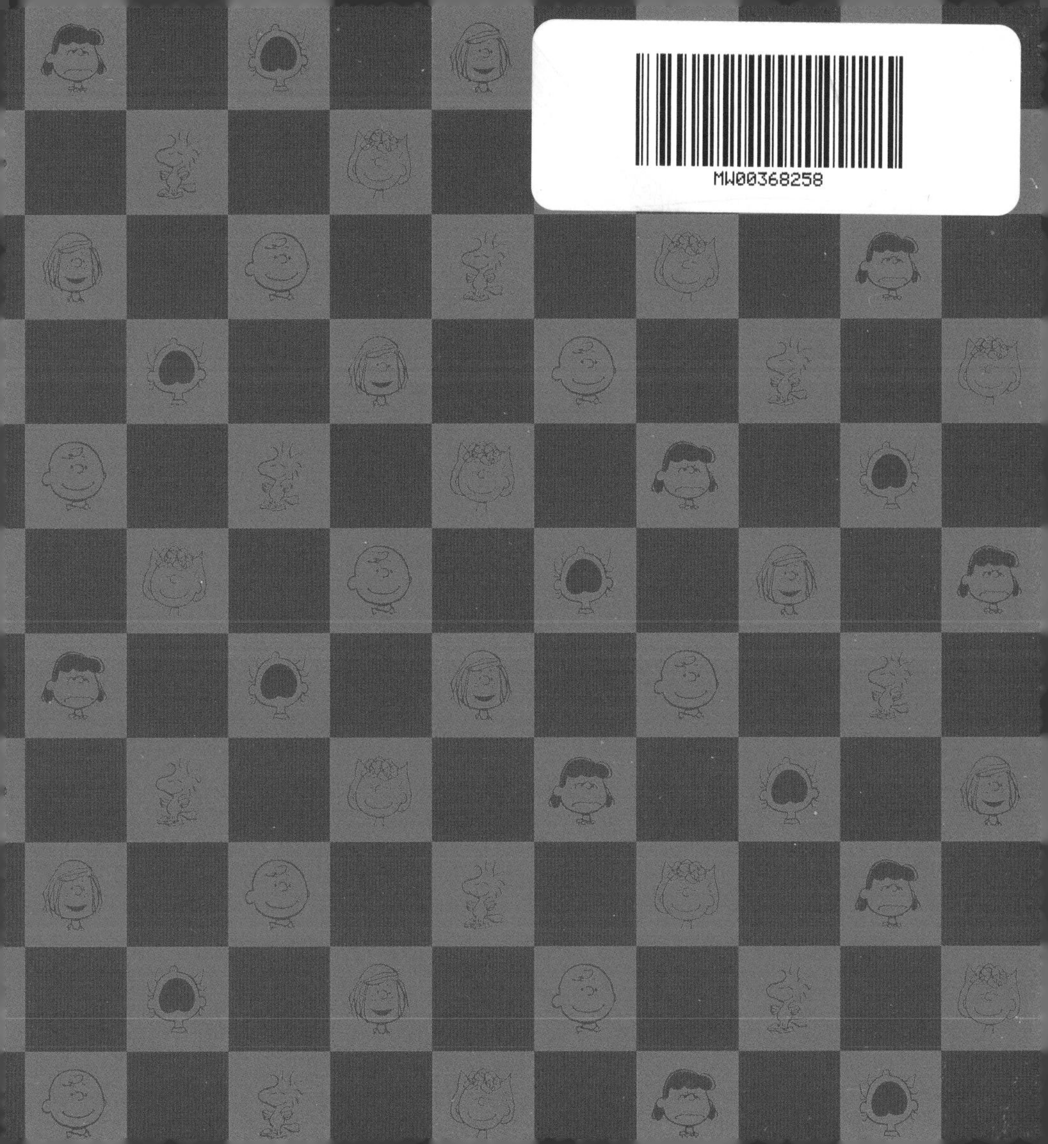

Cheer Up, Charlie Brown!

GETTING THROUGH LIFE ONE LAUGH AT A TIME

Cover and internal design by Michael Franck

Published by Sourcebooks, Inc.
P.O. Box 4410, Naperville, Illinois 60567-4410
(630) 961-3900
Fax: (630) 961-2168

www.sourcebooks.com

Library of Congress Cataloging-in-Publication data is on file with the publisher.

Printed and bound in the United States of America.

WOZ 10 9 8 7 6 5 4 3 2 1

Cheer Up, Charlie Brown!

GETTING THROUGH LIFE ONE LAUGH AT A TIME

Based on the comic strip, PEANUTS, by Charles M. Schulz

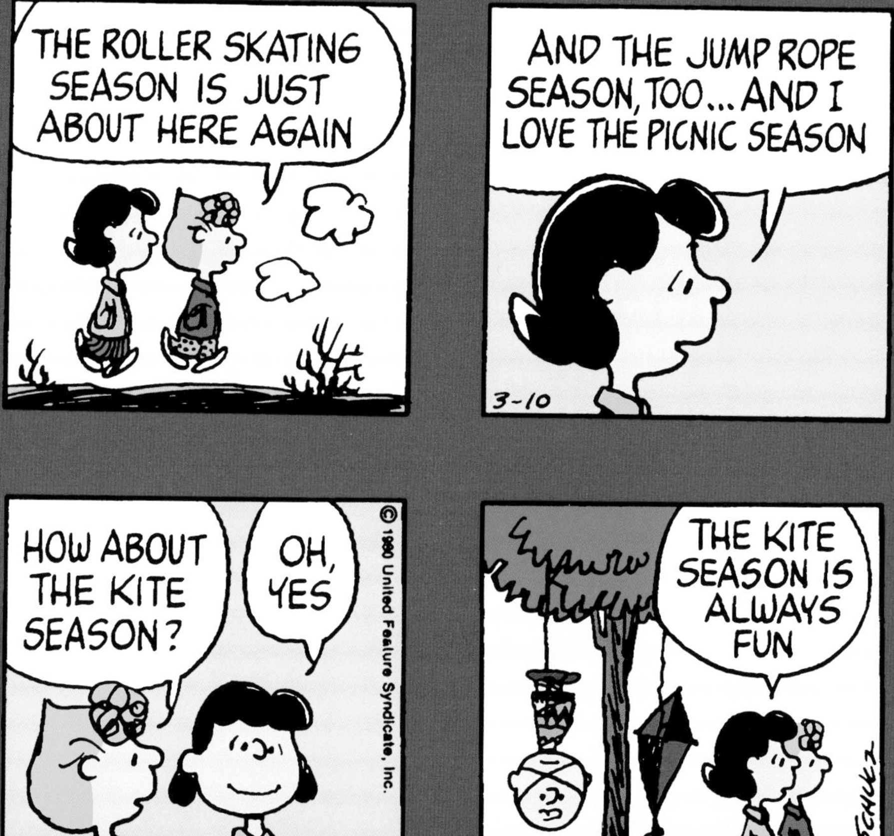
THE ROLLER SKATING SEASON IS JUST ABOUT HERE AGAIN
AND THE JUMP ROPE SEASON, TOO... AND I LOVE THE PICNIC SEASON
3-10
HOW ABOUT THE KITE SEASON?
OH, YES
© 1980 United Feature Syndicate, Inc.
THE KITE SEASON IS ALWAYS FUN
SCHULZ

I did not trip and fall.
I attacked the floor and
I believe I am winning.

— Anonymous

The
road to success
is always
under construction.

— Lily Tomlin

I think I've discovered the
secret of life — you just
hang around
until you get used to it.

— Charles Schulz

In the
book of life,
the answers aren't in the back.

— **Charles Schulz**

Whoever said,
"It's not whether you win
or lose that counts,"
probably lost.

— **Martina Navratilova**

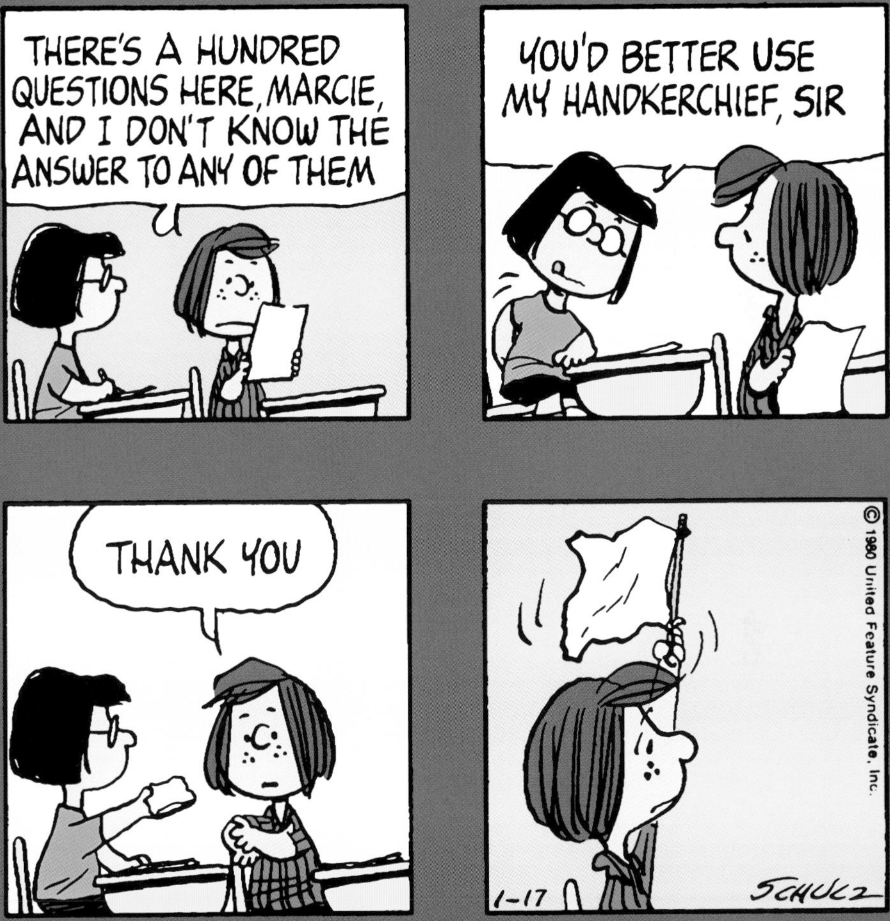
THERE'S A HUNDRED QUESTIONS HERE, MARCIE, AND I DON'T KNOW THE ANSWER TO ANY OF THEM
YOU'D BETTER USE MY HANDKERCHIEF, SIR
THANK YOU
© 1980 United Feature Syndicate, Inc.
1-17
SCHULZ

Sometimes I lie awake at night, and I ask,
"Where have I gone wrong?"
Then a voice says to me,
"This is going to take more than one night."

— Charles Schulz

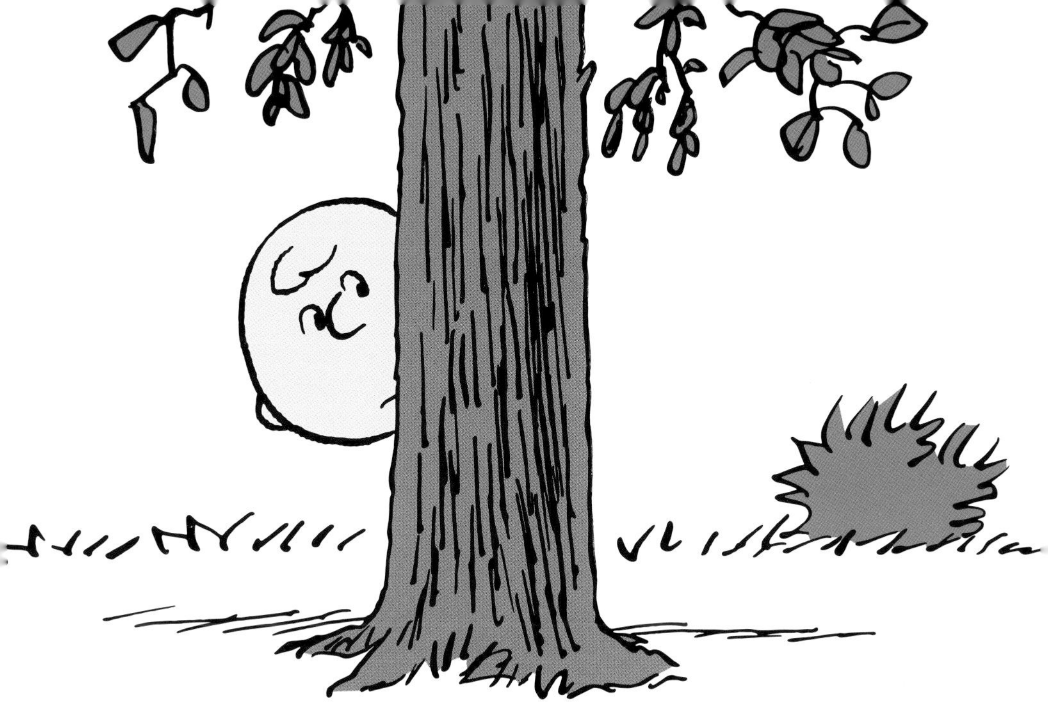

I have a new philosophy.
I'm only going to dread
one day
at a time.

— Charles Schulz

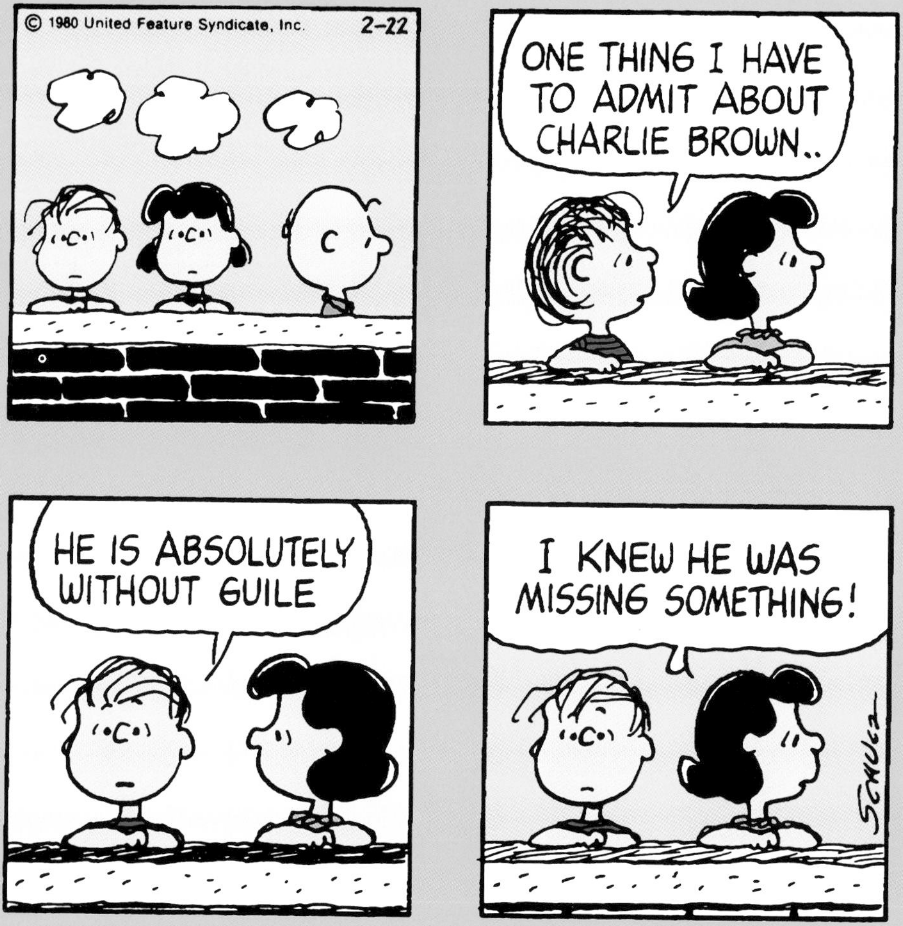

© 1980 United Feature Syndicate, Inc.
2-22
ONE THING I HAVE TO ADMIT ABOUT CHARLIE BROWN..
HE IS ABSOLUTELY WITHOUT GUILE
I KNEW HE WAS MISSING SOMETHING!
SCHULZ

If at first you don't succeed,
failure may be your style.

— Quentin Crisp

Just when I discovered
the meaning of life,
they changed it.

— George Carlin

I told my psychiatrist that
everyone hates me.
He said I was being ridiculous —
everyone hasn't met me yet.

— Rodney Dangerfield

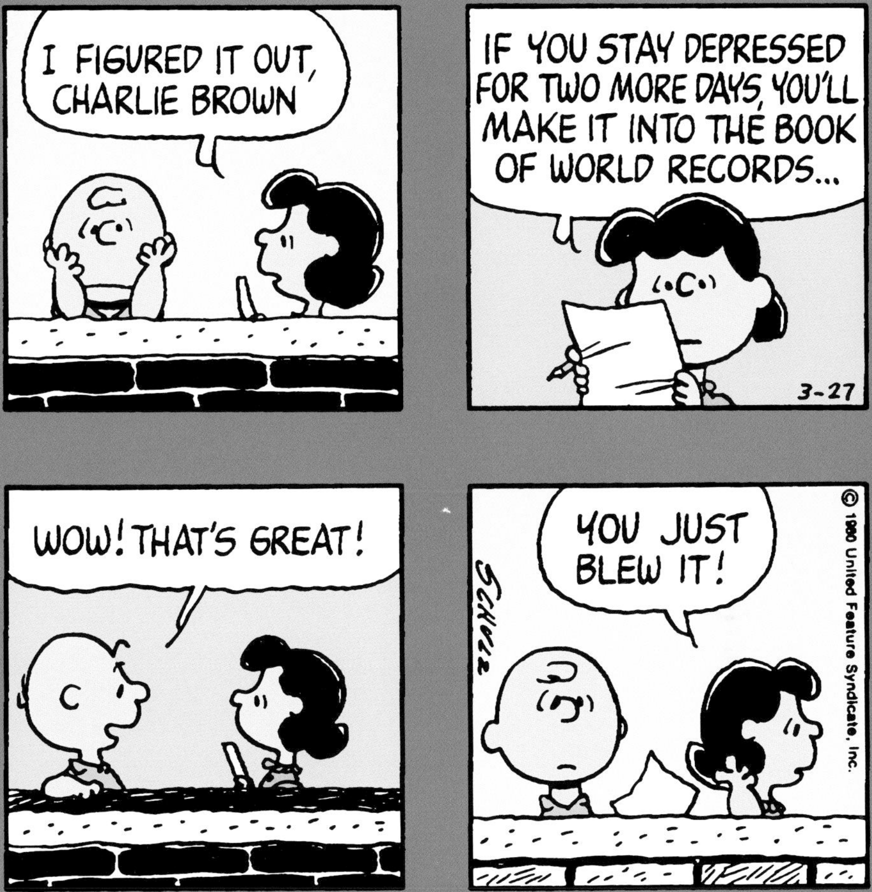
I FIGURED IT OUT, CHARLIE BROWN
IF YOU STAY DEPRESSED FOR TWO MORE DAYS, YOU'LL MAKE IT INTO THE BOOK OF WORLD RECORDS...
3-27
WOW! THAT'S GREAT!
YOU JUST BLEW IT!
SCHULZ
© 1980 United Feature Syndicate, Inc.

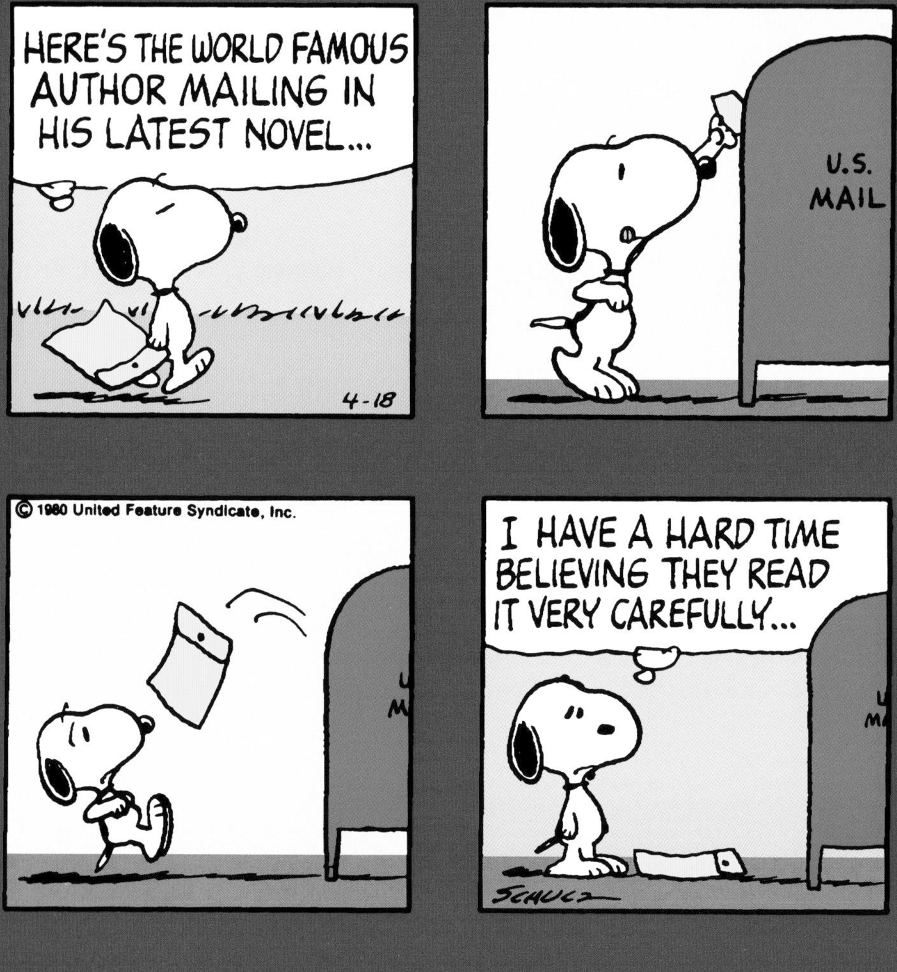
HERE'S THE WORLD FAMOUS AUTHOR MAILING IN HIS LATEST NOVEL...
4-18
U.S. MAIL
© 1980 United Feature Syndicate, Inc.
I HAVE A HARD TIME BELIEVING THEY READ IT VERY CAREFULLY...
SCHULZ

I have not failed.
I've just found
ten thousand ways that
won't work.

— Thomas Edison

Have no fear of
perfection—
you'll never reach it.

— Salvador Dalí

If at first you don't succeed,
destroy all evidence
that you tried.

— Steven Wright

That's the secret to life...

replace one worry with another.

— Charles Schulz

I am so clever that sometimes
I don't understand a
single word
of what I am saying.

— **Oscar Wilde**

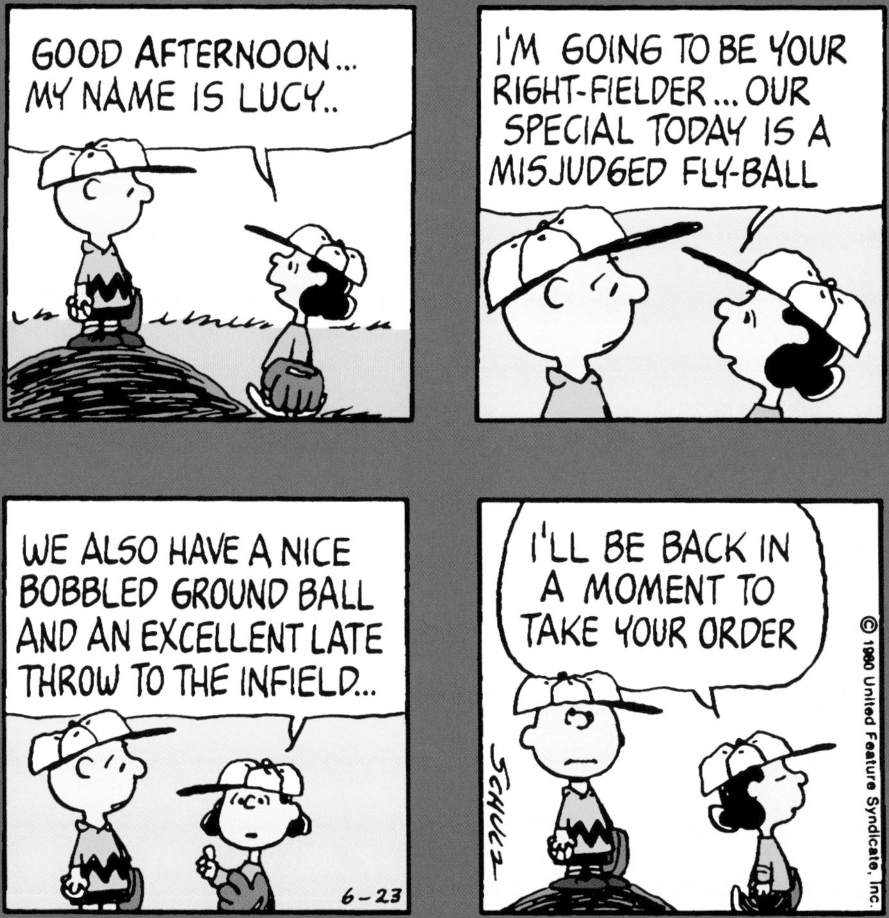
GOOD AFTERNOON... MY NAME IS LUCY..
I'M GOING TO BE YOUR RIGHT-FIELDER... OUR SPECIAL TODAY IS A MISJUDGED FLY-BALL
WE ALSO HAVE A NICE BOBBLED GROUND BALL AND AN EXCELLENT LATE THROW TO THE INFIELD...
6-23
I'LL BE BACK IN A MOMENT TO TAKE YOUR ORDER
SCHULZ
© 1980 United Feature Syndicate, Inc.

Success consists of going from
failure to failure
without loss of
enthusiasm.

— Winston Churchill

I couldn't wait for success,
so I went ahead
without it.

— Jonathan Winters

Just because you're miserable
doesn't mean you can't
enjoy your life.
— **Annette Goodheart**

In the depth of winter I finally
learned that there was in me an
invincible summer.

— **Albert Camus**

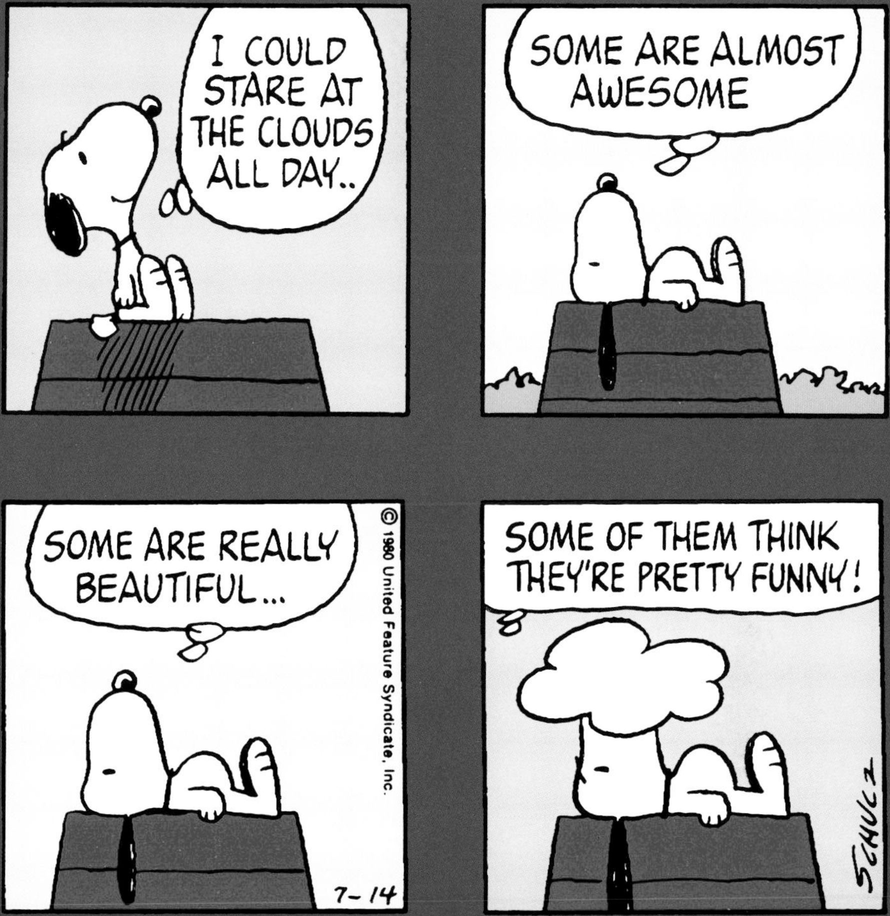
I COULD STARE AT THE CLOUDS ALL DAY..
SOME ARE ALMOST AWESOME
SOME ARE REALLY BEAUTIFUL...
© 1980 United Feature Syndicate, Inc.
7-14
SOME OF THEM THINK THEY'RE PRETTY FUNNY!

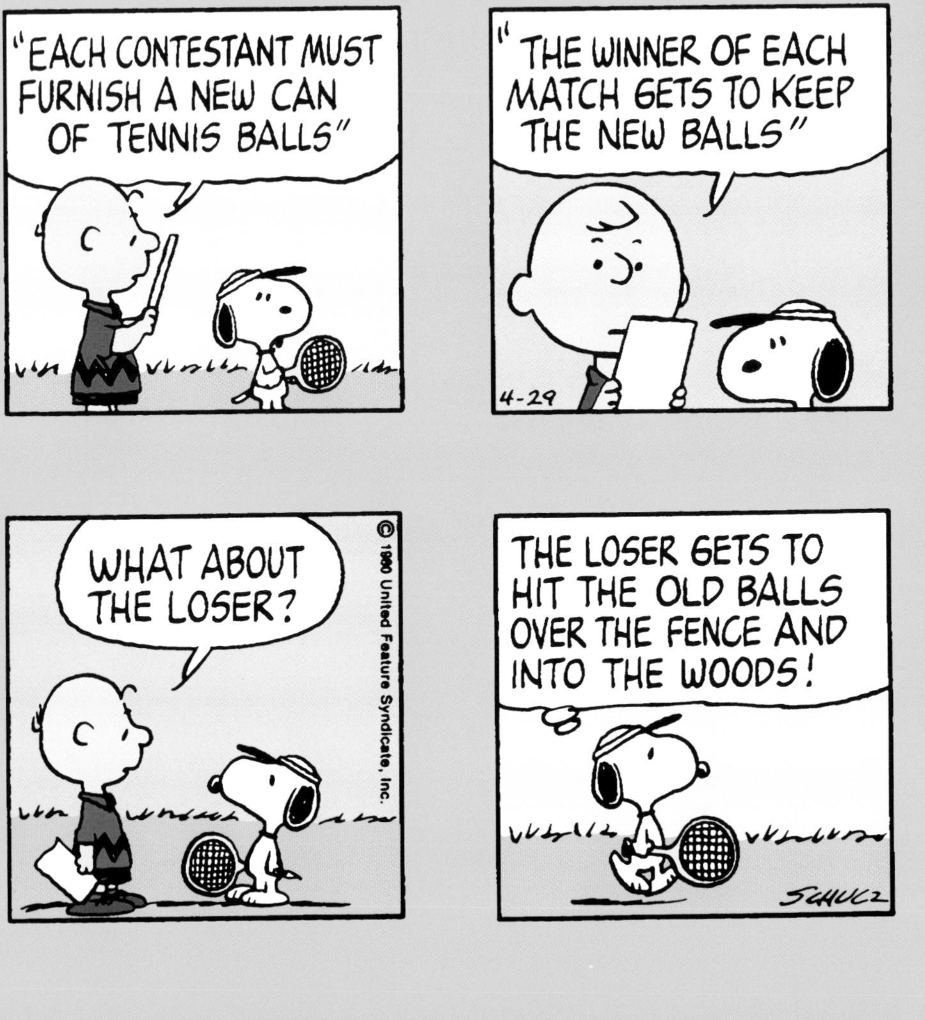
"EACH CONTESTANT MUST FURNISH A NEW CAN OF TENNIS BALLS"
"THE WINNER OF EACH MATCH GETS TO KEEP THE NEW BALLS"
4-29
WHAT ABOUT THE LOSER?
THE LOSER GETS TO HIT THE OLD BALLS OVER THE FENCE AND INTO THE WOODS!
SCHULZ

If winning isn't everything,
why do they keep score?

— Vince Lombardi

You *win* some,
lose some,
and
wreck some.

— Dale Earnhardt

Everything is
funny
as long as it is happening to
somebody else.

— Will Rogers

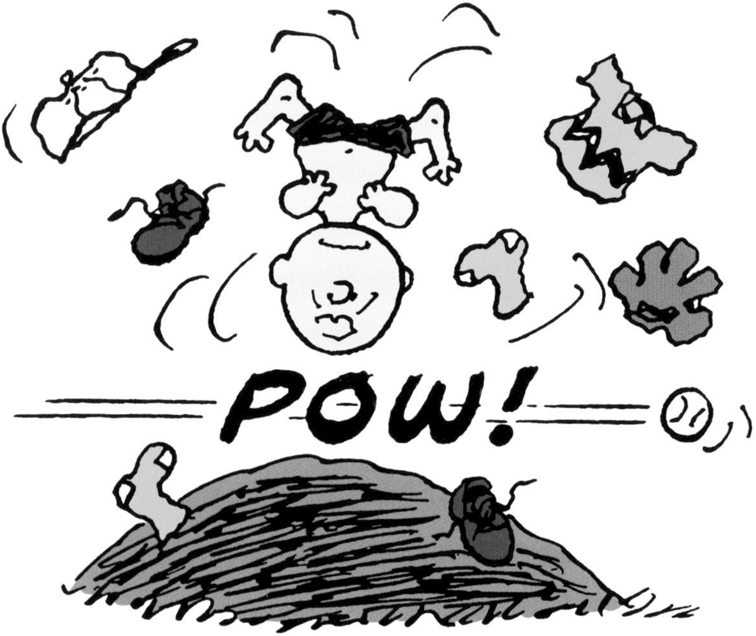
POW!

Go on failing.
Go on.
Only next time, try to
fail better.

— Samuel Beckett

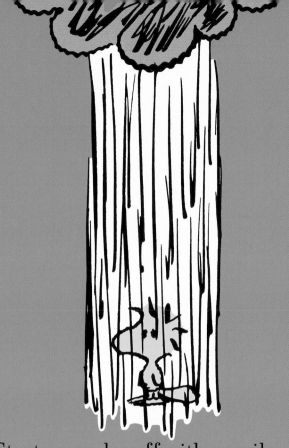

Start every day off with a smile and
get it over with.

— W. C. Fields

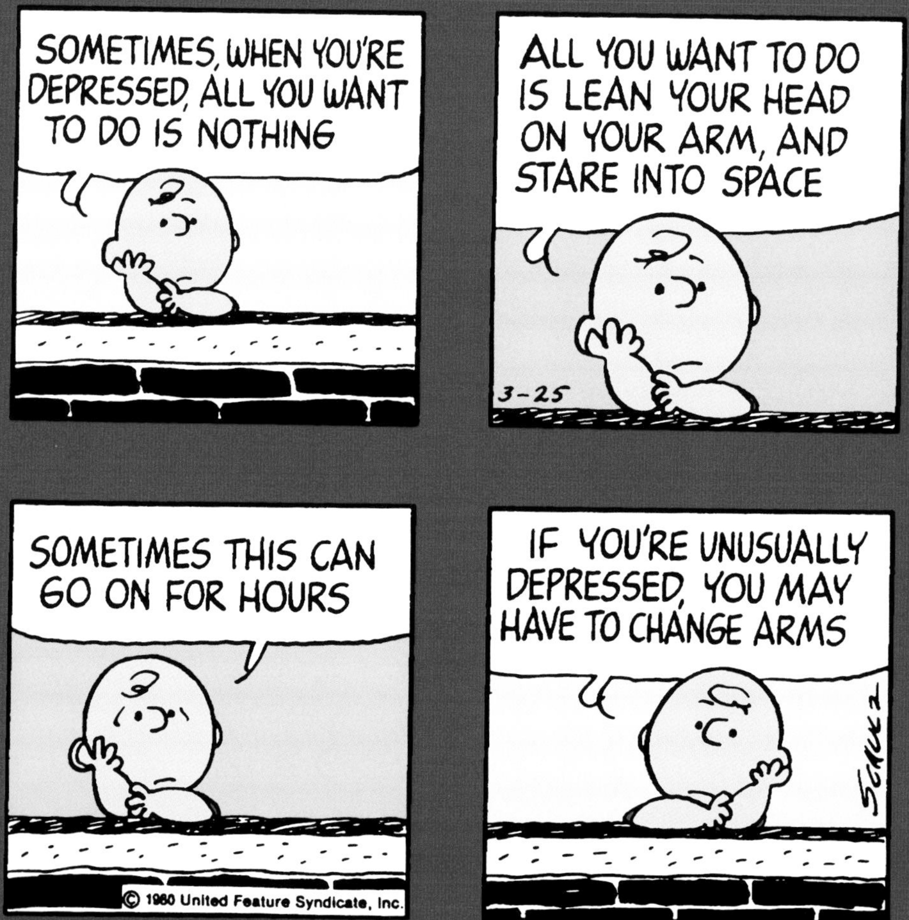
SOMETIMES, WHEN YOU'RE DEPRESSED, ALL YOU WANT TO DO IS NOTHING
ALL YOU WANT TO DO IS LEAN YOUR HEAD ON YOUR ARM, AND STARE INTO SPACE
3-25
SOMETIMES THIS CAN GO ON FOR HOURS
© 1980 United Feature Syndicate, Inc.
IF YOU'RE UNUSUALLY DEPRESSED, YOU MAY HAVE TO CHANGE ARMS
SCHULZ

When you're depressed, it makes
a lot of difference how you stand.
The worst thing you can do is
straighten up and
hold your head high
because then you'll start to feel better.

— **Charles Schulz**

You wouldn't worry so much about
what others think of you
if you realized how seldom they do.

— Eleanor Roosevelt

If only we'd
stop trying
to be happy, we could have a
pretty good time.

— Edith Wharton

Don't wait around for
other people to be happy for you.
Any happiness you get
you've got to make yourself.

— Alice Walker

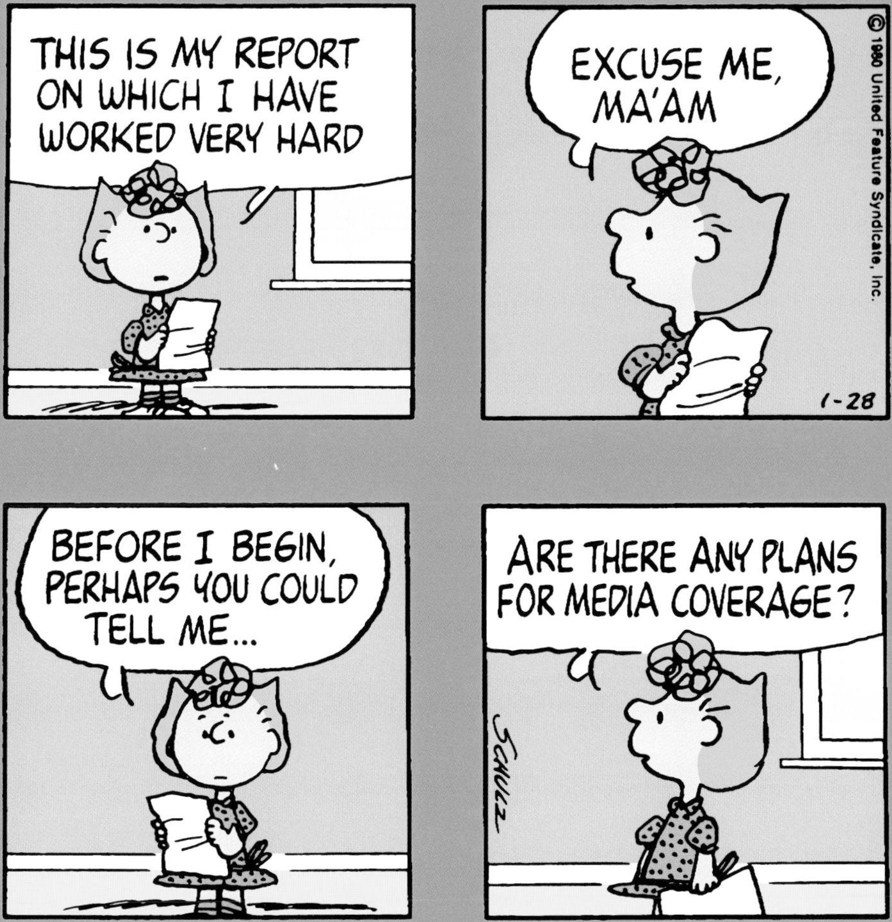
THIS IS MY REPORT ON WHICH I HAVE WORKED VERY HARD
EXCUSE ME, MA'AM
© 1980 United Feature Syndicate, Inc.
1-28
BEFORE I BEGIN, PERHAPS YOU COULD TELL ME...
ARE THERE ANY PLANS FOR MEDIA COVERAGE?
SCHULZ

© 1960 United Feature Syndicate, Inc.
LUCY! HOW IN THE WORLD COULD YOU MISS SUCH AN EASY FLY BALL?
WELL, I THINK IT ALL STARTED RIGHT AFTER I WAS BORN, SEE, WHEN I HAD THIS FEELING OF NOT BEING WANTED, AND...
FORGET IT!
4/19
SCHULZ

Things
turn out best
for people who
make the best
of the way things turn out.

— **John Wooden**

In times like these,
it helps to recall that
there have always been
times like these.

— **Paul Harvey**

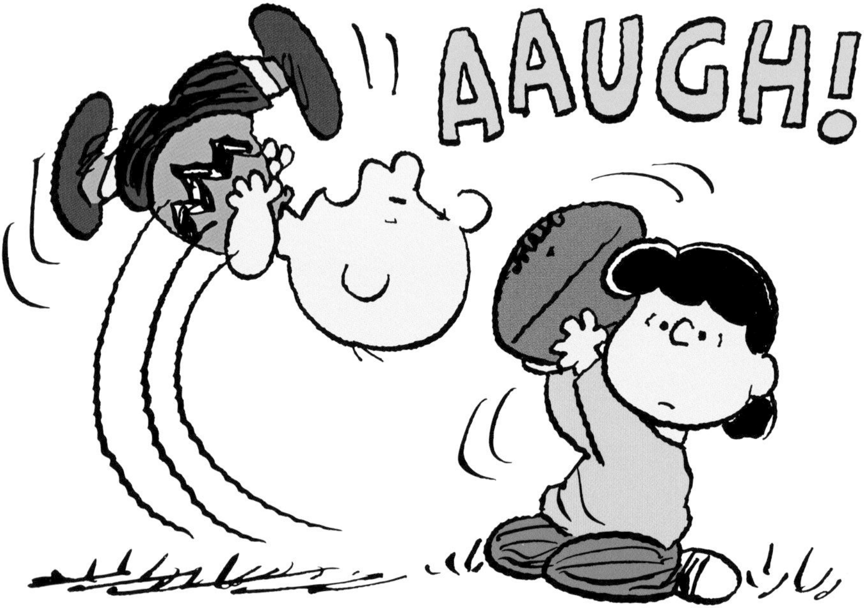
AAUGH!

I honestly think it is better to be a failure at
something you love
than to be a success at
something you hate.

— George Burns

The **art of living** is more like **wrestling** than **dancing.**

— Marcus Aurelius

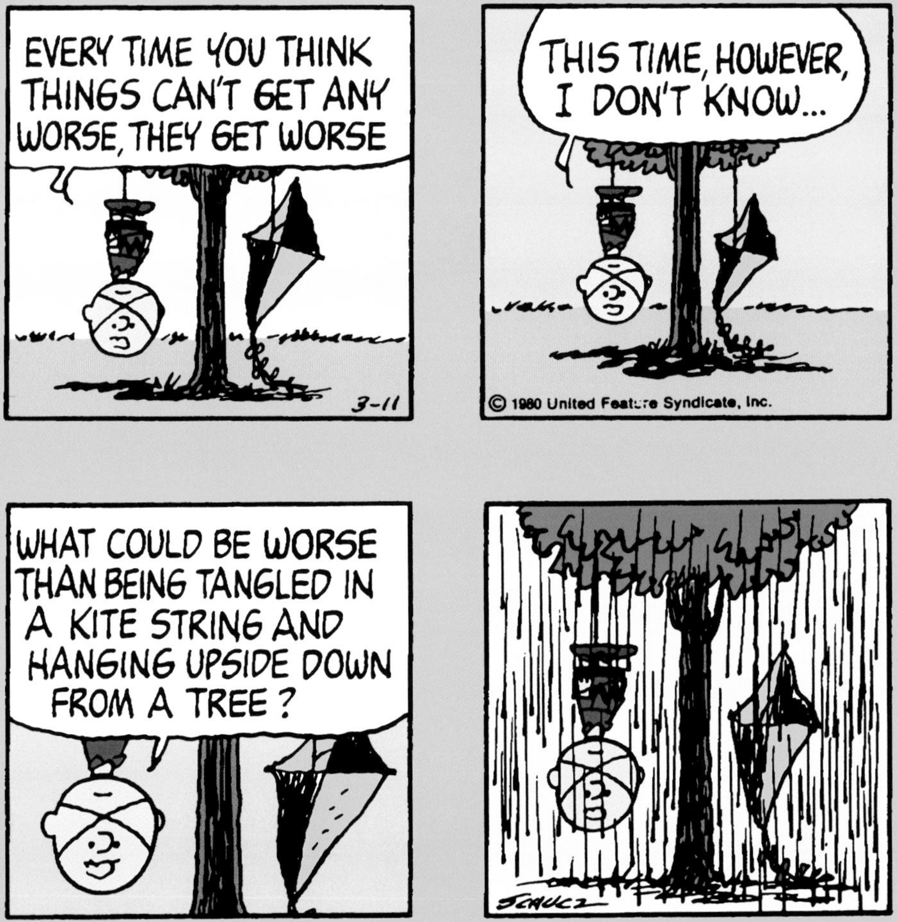

EVERY TIME YOU THINK THINGS CAN'T GET ANY WORSE, THEY GET WORSE
3-11
THIS TIME, HOWEVER, I DON'T KNOW...
© 1980 United Feature Syndicate, Inc.
WHAT COULD BE WORSE THAN BEING TANGLED IN A KITE STRING AND HANGING UPSIDE DOWN FROM A TREE ?
SCHULZ

The difference between
life and the movies
is that a script has
to make sense, and
life doesn't.

— Joseph Mankiewicz

If you're going through hell,
keep going.

— Winston Churchill

Sometimes you're the **windshield;** sometimes you're the *bug.*

— **Mark Knopfler**

If you know you are going to fail, then **fail gloriously!**

— **Cate Blanchett**

If at first you **don't succeed,** find out if the loser gets anything.

— **William Lyon Phelps**

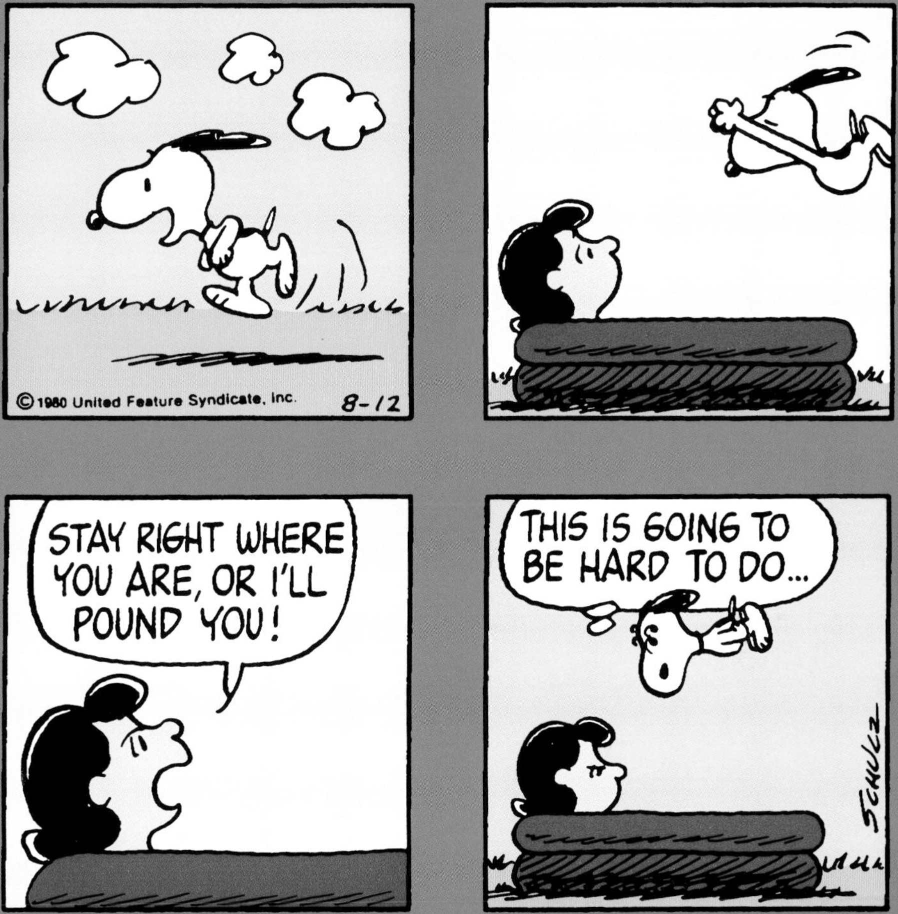
© 1980 United Feature Syndicate, Inc.
8-12
STAY RIGHT WHERE YOU ARE, OR I'LL POUND YOU!
THIS IS GOING TO BE HARD TO DO...
SCHULZ

LIFE IS A LOT LIKE A BASEBALL GAME
WE ALL HAVE CERTAIN POSITIONS THAT WE PLAY
8-9
WE ALL MAKE A FEW HITS AND WE ALL MAKE A FEW ERRORS
HOW MANY INNINGS ARE WE PLAYING?
SCHULZ
© 1980 United Feature Syndicate, Inc.

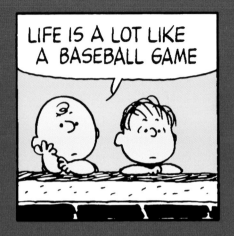

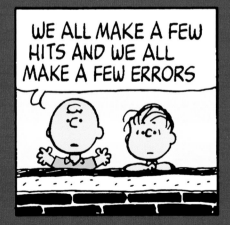

I've had a wonderful time, but
this wasn't it.

— Groucho Marx

It always looks
darkest
just before it gets
totally black.

— Charles Schulz

I'm tired of following my dreams.
I'm just going to ask them
where they're going,
and
hook up with them later.

— Mitch Hedberg

Not a **shred of evidence** exists in favor of the idea that life is serious.

— Brendan Gill

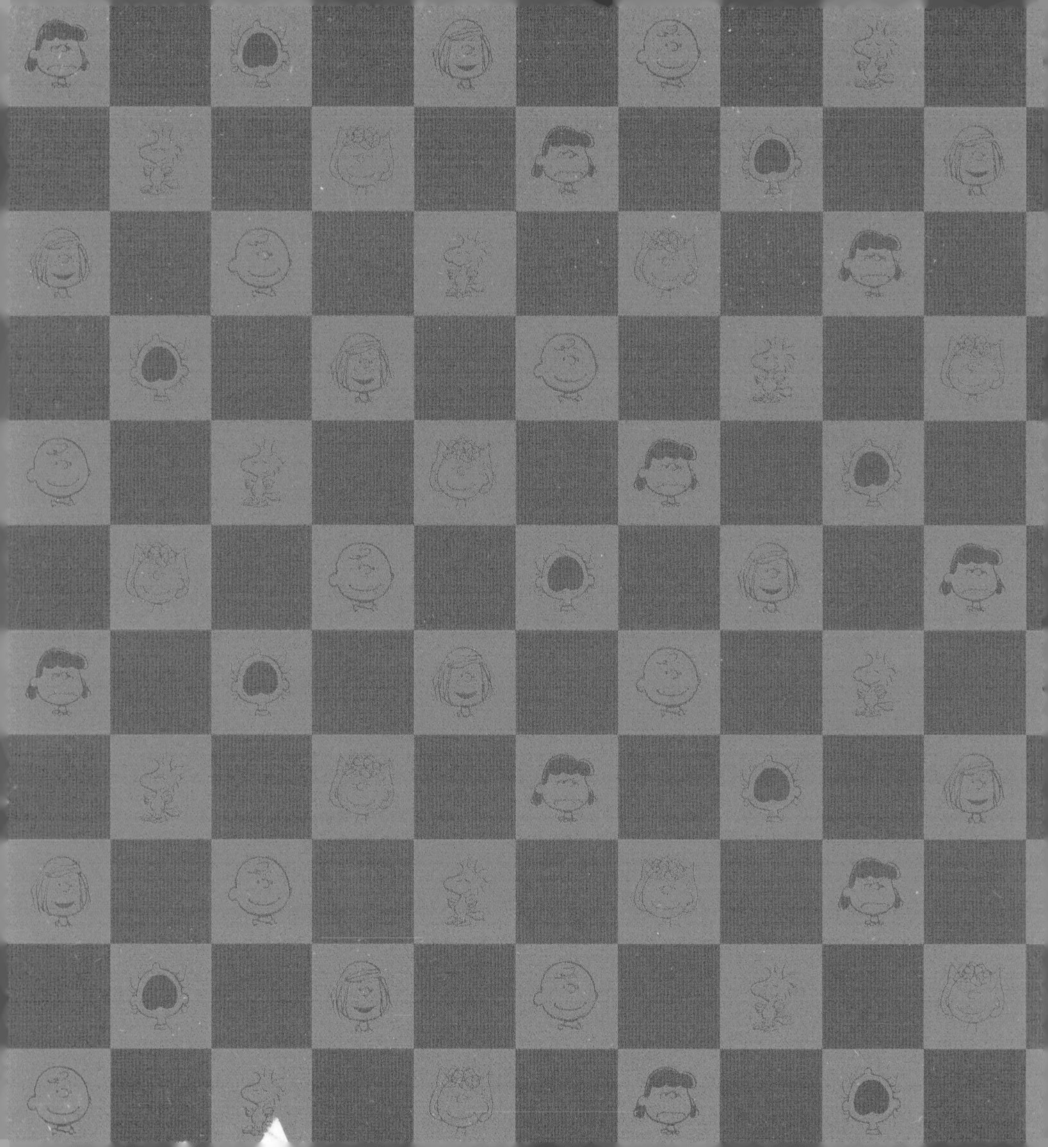